To:_____

From:_____

*M*ay Jesus, our Savior,
   who was born on Christmas Day,
Bless you at this season
   in a very special way.
May the beauty and the promise
   of that silent, holy night
Fill your heart with peace and happiness
   and make your New Year bright.

THE HELEN STEINER RICE FOUNDATION

*G*od knows no strangers, He loves us all,
The poor, the rich, the great, the small.
He is a Friend who is always there
To share our troubles and lessen our care.
No one is a stranger in God's sight,
For God is love and in His light
May we, too, try in our small way
To make new friends from day to day.

Whatever the celebration, whatever the day, whatever the event, whatever the occasion, Helen Steiner Rice possessed the ability to express the appropriate feeling for that particular moment in time.

A happening became happier, a sentiment more sentimental, a memory more memorable because of her deep sensitivity to put into understandable language the emotion being experienced. Her positive attitude, her concern for others, and her love of God are identifiable threads woven into her life, her work . . . and even her death.

Prior to Mrs. Rice's passing, she established the HELEN STEINER RICE FOUNDATION, a nonprofit corporation that awards grants to worthy charitable programs that aid the elderly and the needy.

Royalties from the sale of this book will add to the financial capabilities of the HELEN STEINER RICE FOUNDATION. Because of limited resources, the foundation presently limits grants to qualified charitable programs in Lorain, Ohio, where Helen Steiner Rice was born, and Greater Cincinnati, Ohio, where Mrs. Rice lived and worked most of her life. Hopefully in the future resources will be of sufficient size that broader areas can be considered in the awarding of grants. Thank you for your assistance in helping to keep Helen's dream alive and growing.

Andrea R. Cornett, Administrator

Virginia J. Ruehlmann has compiled over thirty books using Mrs. Rice's inspirational poems. Mrs. Ruehlmann is also the author of *Making Family Memories: Crafts and Activities.*

Stan Myers is an award-winning artist and member of the prestigious National Watercolor Society. His work is included in both private and corporate collections, and represented by several galleries in the Midwest.

Christmas Blessings

HELEN STEINER RICE

Compiled by Virginia J. Ruehlmann

Gramercy Books
New York

Copyright © 1991, 1996 by Virginia J. Ruehlmann and
The Helen Steiner Rice Foundation
All rights reserved under International and Pan-American
Copyright Conventions.

Scripture quotations are from the Revised Standard Version of the Bible,
copyright © 1946, 1952, 1971, 1973
by the Division of Christian Education of the National Council of the Churches of Christ
in the United States of America.

This 2000 edition is published by Gramercy Books™,
an imprint of Random House Value Publishing, Inc.,
280 Park Avenue, New York, New York 10017,
by arrangement with Fleming H. Revell, a division of Baker Book House Company.

Gramercy Books™ and design are trademarks of
Random House Value Publishing, Inc.

Random House
New York • Toronto • London • Sydney • Auckland
http://www.randomhouse.com/

Jacket and interior illustrations by Stan Myers

Printed and bound in the United States of America

A CIP catalog record for this book is available from the Library of Congress.

ISBN 0-517-20871-7

8 7 6 5 4 3 2 1

Dedicated to

fans, friends, family,
former co-workers, and neighbors
of Helen Steiner Rice
and
especially and gratefully
to her sister,
Gertrude Steiner,

in memory of the many Christmases shared

Contents

Introduction

Christmas, that most beautiful and highly cherished feast of the Christian year, is celebrated in remembrance of the nativity of our Lord.

Unfortunately, there are times when the true meaning of Christmas is lost in the hustle-bustle-hurry-scurry days of December.

The role Christmas plays in an individual's life depends on the interpretation of the event and varies from person to person and family to family. There are, however, certain qualities of Christmas, such as the miracle and spirit of the day, its effect, its glory, and its joy, that are appreciated by all believers. To promote, promulgate, and pass these values on from generation to generation should be the goal of each Christian.

Helen Steiner Rice understood this challenge. She grasped these qualities and beautifully expressed them in her works, in heartwarming sentiments and easy to comprehend terms.

May this collection of her verses assist you in capturing and retaining the true meaning of Christmas, its values, and the enjoyment that can radiate from it.

Virginia J. Ruehlmann

The Miracle of Christ's Birth

Christmas is the miracle of Christ's birth—
a virgin conceiving, miraculous and amazing,
a star shining, angels praising,
shepherds kneeling, throngs adoring,
joy increasing, spirits soaring.

VJR

*N*ow the birth of Jesus Christ took place in this way. When his mother Mary had been betrothed to Joseph, before they came together she was found to be with child of the Holy Spirit; and her husband Joseph, being a just man and unwilling to put her to shame, resolved to divorce her quietly. But as he considered this, behold, an angel of the Lord appeared to him in a dream, saying, "Joseph, son of David, do not fear to take Mary your wife, for that which is conceived in her is of the Holy Spirit; she will bear a son, and you shall call his name Jesus, for he will save his people from their sins." All this took place to fulfil what the Lord had spoken by the prophet:

> "Behold, a virgin shall conceive and bear a son,
> and his name shall be called Emmanuel"

(which means, God with us). When Joseph woke from sleep, he did as the angel of the Lord commanded him; he took his wife, but knew her not until she had borne a son; and he called his name Jesus.

Matthew 1:18–25

Unto Us a Child Is Born

God sent the little Christ child
    so men might understand
That a little child shall lead them
    to that unknown Promised Land.
For God in His great wisdom
    knew that men would rise to power
And forget His holy precepts
    in their great triumphal hour.
He knew that they would question
    and doubt the holy birth
And turn their time and talents
    to the pleasures of this earth.

But every new discovery
    is an open avenue
To more and greater mysteries,
    and man's search is never through.
For man can never fathom
    the mysteries of the Lord
Or understand His promise
    of a heavenly reward.
For no one but a little child
    with simple faith and love
Can lead man's straying footsteps
    to higher realms above!

May the Blessings of Christmas Be Yours

The blessings of Christmas are many,
    more than words can express,
Enough to fill every longing heart
    with untold happiness.
And the greatest of all blessings
    is the Christmas revelation
That Jesus Christ was born this day
    to bring the world salvation.
And that is why this message
    is written here to say
That you are wished the blessings
    of the holy Christmas Day.

Was It Really So?

A star in the sky, an angel's voice
Telling the world—Rejoice! Rejoice!
But that was centuries and centuries ago,
And we ask today was it really so?
Was the Christ child born in a manger bed
Without a pillow to rest His head?
Did He walk on earth and live and die
And return to God to dwell on high?
We were not there to hear or see,
But our hopes and dreams of eternity
Are centered around that holy story
When God sent us His Son in glory.
And life on earth has not been the same,
Regardless of what the skeptics claim,
For no event ever left behind
A transformation of this kind.
So question and search and doubt, if you will,
But the story of Christmas is living still.

God, Make Us Aware

God, make us aware
    that in Thy name
The holy Christ child
    humbly came
To live on earth
    and leave behind
New faith and hope
    for all mankind.
And make us aware
    that the Christmas story
Is everyone's promise
    of eternal glory.

The First Christmas Morn

In this world of violence
    and hatred and greed
Where men lust for power
    and scorn those in need,
What could we hope for
    and where could we go
To find comfort and courage
    on this earth below
If in Bethlehem's manger
    Christ had not been born
Many centuries ago
    on the first Christmas morn?
For life everlasting
    and eternal glory
Were promised to man
    in the Christmas story!

The Wonder of Christmas

The wonderment in a small child's eyes,
The ageless awe in the Christmas skies,
The nameless joy that fills the air,
The throngs that kneel in praise and prayer . . .
These are the things that make us know
That men may come and men may go,
But none will ever find a way
To banish Christ from Christmas Day,
For with each child there's born again
A mystery that baffles men.

The Peace
of Faith

Christmas is the peace of faith—
bells ringing, folks churchgoing,
choirs singing, warm wishes flowing,
joy to the world and silent nighting,
peace on earth, calm and quieting.

VJR

*T*herefore the Lord himself will give you a sign. Behold, a young woman shall conceive and bear a son, and shall call his name Immanuel.

Isaiah 7:14

For to us a child is born,
    to us a son is given;
and the government will be upon his shoulder,
    and his name will be called
"Wonderful Counselor, Mighty God,
    Everlasting Father, Prince of Peace."

Isaiah 9:6

But you, O Bethlehem Ephrathah,
    who are little to be among the clans of Judah,
from you shall come forth for me
    one who is to be ruler in Israel,
whose origin is from of old,
    from ancient days.

Micah 5:2

The Miracle of Christmas

Miracles are marvels
    that defy all explanation,
And Christmas is a miracle
    and not just a celebration.
For when the true significance
    of this so-called Christmas story
Penetrates the minds of men
    and transforms them with its glory,
Then only can rebellious man
    so hate-torn with dissension
Behold his adversaries
    with a broader new dimension—
And that is why God sent His Son
    as a Christmas gift of love
So that wickedness and hatred,
    which the world had so much of,
Could find another outlet
    by following in Christ's way
And discovering a new power
    that violence can't outweigh.

May Christ Be Reborn in Our Hearts

We've come a long way since that first Christmas night
When led by a star so wondrously bright
The wise men journeyed to find the place
That cradled the Christ child's beautiful face.
But like lost sheep we have wandered away
From God and His Son, who was born Christmas Day,
And instead of depending on God's guiding hand
Ingenious man has assumed full command
Like the prodigal son who seeks to be free
From the heavenly Father and His holy decree.
But life without God is corroding man's soul,
Weakening his spirit and distorting his goal,
And unless we return to our Father again,
We will never have peace and goodwill among men,
And the freedom man sought will make him a slave
For only through God is man strong, free, and brave.
So let us return to our Father and pray
That Christ is reborn in our hearts Christmas Day.

What Is Christmas?

Is it just a day at the end of the year,
A holiday filled with merry good cheer,
A season for presents—both taking and giving,
A time to indulge in the pleasures of living?
Are we lost in a meaningless, much-muddled daze
That covers our minds like a gray autumn haze?
Have we closed our hearts to God and His love,
And turned our eyes from the bright star above?
O Father in heaven, renew and restore
The real, true meaning of Christmas once more,
So we can feel in our hearts again
That "Peace on earth, goodwill to men"
Is still a promise that we can claim
If we but seek it in Thy name.

Faith

Unless you become as children
    and love Me as they do,
You cannot enter My kingdom,
    for the door is closed to you.
For faith is the key to heaven
    and only God's children hold
The key that opens the gateway
    to that beautiful City of Gold.
For only a child yet unblemished
    by the doctrines and theories of man
Is content to trust and love Jesus
    without understanding His plan.

God, Grant Us Hope
and Faith and Love

Hope for a world grown cynically cold,
Hungry for power and greedy for gold—
Faith to believe when, within and without,
There's a nameless fear in a world of doubt—
Love that is bigger than race or creed
To cover the world and fulfill each need . . .
God, grant these gifts to all troubled hearts
As the old year ends and a new year starts.

Christmas

C is for the Christ child,
 a child of love and light

H is for the Heavens that were
 bright that holy night

R is for the Radiance
 of the star that led the way

I is for the lowly Inn
 where the infant Jesus lay

S is for the Shepherds
 who beheld the Christmas star

T is for the Tidings
 the angels told afar

M is for the Magi
 with their gifts of myrrh and gold

A is for the Angels
 who were awesome to behold

S is for the Savior
 who was born to save all men

And together this spells *CHRISTMAS*,
 which we celebrate again.

A Christmas Prayer for Peace

We pray to Thee, our Father,
    as Christmas comes again,
For peace among all nations
    and goodwill among all men.
Give us strength and courage
    to search ourselves inside
And recognize our vanity,
    our selfishness, and pride.
For the struggle of all ages
    is centered deep within
Where each man has a private war
    that his own soul must win.
For a world of peace and plenty,
    of which all men have dreamed,
Can only be attained and kept
    when the spirit is redeemed.

Glory to God in the Highest

"Glory to God in the highest
        and peace on earth to men"—
May the Christmas song the angels sang
        stir in our hearts again
And bring a new awareness
        that the fate of every nation
Is sealed securely in the hand
        of the Maker of creation.
For man, with all his knowledge,
        his inventions, and his skill,
Can never go an inch beyond
        the holy Father's will,
For greater than the scope of man
        and far beyond all seeing,
In Him who made the universe,
        man lives and has his being.

The Warmth of Friendships

*C*hristmas is the warmth of friendships—
letter writing, card sending,
news exciting, goodwill extending,
neighbors gathering, friendly greetings,
manger scenes, community meetings.

VJR

The angel Gabriel was sent from God to a city of Galilee named Nazareth, to a virgin betrothed to a man whose name was Joseph, of the house of David; and the virgin's name was Mary. And he came to her and said, "Hail, O favored one, the Lord is with you!" But she was greatly troubled at the saying, and considered in her mind what sort of greeting this might be. And the angel said to her, "Do not be afraid, Mary, for you have found favor with God. And behold, you will conceive in your womb and bear a son, and you shall call his name Jesus.

He will be great, and will be called the Son of the Most High;
and the Lord God will give to him the throne of his father David,
and he will reign over the house of Jacob for ever;
and of his kingdom there will be no end."

And Mary said to the angel, "How shall this be, since I have no husband?" And the angel said to her,

"The Holy Spirit will come upon you,
and the power of the Most High will overshadow you;
therefore the child to be born will be called holy,
the Son of God."

Luke 1:26–35

A Christmas Message

Love is like magic
  and it always will be,
For love still remains
  life's sweet mystery.
Love works in ways
  that are wondrous and strange
And there's nothing in life
  that love cannot change.
Love can transform
  the most commonplace
Into beauty and splendor
  and sweetness and grace.
Love is unselfish,
  understanding, and kind,
For it sees with its heart
  and not with its mind.
Love is the answer
  that everyone seeks;
Love is the language
  that every heart speaks.
Love is the message
  that was sent to the earth
On that first holy Christmas
  that heralded Christ's birth!

Gift of Friendship

When you ask God for a gift,
   be thankful if He sends
Not diamonds, pearls, and riches
   but the love of real true friends.

Christmastime Is Friendship Time

At Christmastime our hearts reach out
  to friends we think of dearly,
And checking through our friendship lists,
  as all of us do yearly,
We stop awhile to reminisce
  and to pleasantly review
Happy little happenings
  and things we used to do,
And though we've been too busy
  to keep in touch all year,
We send a Christmas greeting
  at this season of good cheer.
So Christmas is a lovely link
  between old years and new
That keeps the bond of friendship
  forever unbroken and true.

*H*elen Steiner Rice enjoyed keeping in touch with her many fans and friends. Each Christmastime she composed and sent special greetings to those on her list. Reminisce as you read the sentiments she expressed in those messages throughout the years.

*M*ay Christmas this year, amid chaos, cruelty, and conflict, be a blessed instrument through which we can find comfort and courage and cheer in the communion of our hearts.

May we discover this Christmas the sustaining powers of a strong faith and the abiding values of courage, heroism, honor, fellowship, and freedom.

May our material gifts be less and our spiritual gifts greater.

"Peace on earth, goodwill to men" is not an empty dream, it is the miracle of Christmas—and such miracles are made of faith and brave hearts.

May God bless America and you, and may the New Year find us all not only safe but free.

Helen Steiner Rice
Christmas, 1942

*I*n a world grown weary with war, Christmas shines out like a candle of courage and comfort amid the darkness of destruction.

Nineteen hundred and forty-four years ago the world heard the words "Peace on earth, goodwill toward men," and as we await another Christmas, it is with a gleam of hope that God will grant the fulfillment of this message that has been ringing down through the years.

May this Christmas be a beacon light to a better world, and may the New Year bring us peace, founded in freedom, and grant us the strength born of suffering to build a world that war can never touch again.

Helen Steiner Rice
Christmas, 1944

I have a list of folks I know, all written in a book,
And every year when Christmas comes, I go and take a look,
And that is when I realize that these names are a part,
Not of the book they're written in, but of my very heart.
For each name stands for someone who has crossed my path sometime,
And in that meeting they've become the rhythm in each rhyme,
And while it sounds fantastic for me to make this claim,
I really feel that I'm composed of each remembered name.
And while you may not be aware of any special link,
Just meeting you has shaped my life a lot more than you think,
For once I've met somebody, the years cannot erase
The memory of a pleasant word or of a friendly face.
So never think my Christmas cards are just a mere routine,
Of names upon a Christmas list, forgotten in between,
For when I send a Christmas card that is addressed to you,
It's because you're on that list of folks whom I'm indebted to.
For I am but the total of the many folks I've met,
And you happen to be one of those I prefer not to forget,
For if I've known you many years or only just a few,
In some way, be it large or small, I owe myself to you.
And every year when Christmas comes, I realize anew,
The best gift life can offer is meeting folks like you.
So Merry, Merry Christmas and no words can suffice,
To say how much your friendship means to

Helen Steiner Rice
Christmas, 1949

42

*A*gain it's Christmas and the year's at an end,
And once again it is time to send
Greetings and gifts and words of cheer
To those whom we know and those we hold dear.
And so I come as in years before
To knock again on your heart's door,
And I say "heart's door" as no figure of speech
But because it's your heart that I want to reach,
For unless the door of your heart swings wide
This message I send you at Christmastide
Is nothing more than an artist's design,
Bringing a few rhyming words of mine.
But these words I write you are meant to be
Much more than a casual greeting from me,
They come each year as a symbol of
The great Christmas gift that was given for love
That all too often is hidden from view
In the glamorized, advertised hullabaloo.

So my wish for you is not gifts of gold
That you can unwrap for the world to behold,
But I'm hoping your home and heart are bright,
Not with glittering gifts, but an inner light,
For the lights of Christmas are not on a tree,
They're deep in the hearts of you and me.
And I want you to know that it's folks like you
Who light lights in my heart and other hearts too,
And my heart reaches out to yours today
With a wish too big for small words to say,
A wish that the meaning of Christmas will stay
And light candles of love that will not fade away
But will glow in your heart and home all year
And light all the lives that you come near—
For the light of the world can only be lit
By the lights in the hearts that are part of it.

Helen Steiner Rice
Christmas, 1952

*I*t's Christmas and time to greet you once more,
But what can I say that I've not said before
Except to repeat at this meaningful season
That I have a deeply significant reason
For sending this greeting to tell you today
How thankful I am that you passed my way
For I happen to have a deep feeling love
For even the people I know little of.
The stranger who smiles as we pass on the street
Or the business acquaintance I happen to meet
Are more than just people with a name and a face,
They are part of God's love and each one has a place
In the plan of our Father which is much greater than
All of the plans and inventions of man.
And so may the knowledge that God's everywhere,
And as close to you always as one little prayer,
Help you to know that you're never alone,
For God is your Father and you're one of His own.
And may Christmas bring you a lovely heart lift
And may Christ Himself be your Christmas gift.

Helen Steiner Rice
Christmas, 1956

$\mathcal{T}$he years bring many changes in many ways, it's true,
And perhaps I should change and modernize too,
Perhaps I should stop sending long Christmas rhymes
And change to a greeting more in tune with the times,
Something that's casual and impersonally terse,
Instead of a warm little heart-to-heart verse,
For I have been told that in this modern day
A heart-to-heart greeting is strictly passé.
But I can't help feeling there's already too much
Of that heartlessly cold and impersonal touch
In business and all walks of living today
And nothing remains to brighten our way,
For what is there left to make the heart sing
When life is a cold and mechanical thing,
And what have we won if in reaching this goal
We gain the whole world and lose our own soul?
And so, though I'm open to much ridicule
As one who belongs to an outmoded school,
I still am convinced that kindness, not force,
Is the wiser and better and more Christlike course.

For no modern world of controlled automation
No matter how perfect its regimentation
Can ever bring joy or peace to the earth
Or fulfill the promise of Jesus Christ's birth,
For progress, and money, and buttons to press,
And comfort and leisure and toil that is less
Cannot by themselves make a world that is free
Where all live together in true harmony.
For it isn't the progress made by man's mind
But a sensitive heart that is generous and kind
That can lighten life's burden and soften life's sorrow
And open the way to a better tomorrow.
And a better tomorrow is my wish and my prayer
Not only for you but for folks everywhere,
And I hope that this Christmas will bring you and yours
The joy that's eternal and the peace that endures.
But with life's many changes one fact remains true,
I'm richer for having known someone like you.

Helen Steiner Rice
Christmas, 1957

*O*ur Father, up in heaven,
    hear this Christmas prayer:
May the people of all nations
    be united in Thy care,
For earth's peace and man's salvation
    can come only by Thy grace
And not through bombs and missiles
    and our quest for outer space.
For until all men recognize
    that the battle is the Lord's
And peace on earth cannot be won
    with strategy and swords,
We will go on vainly fighting,
    as we have in ages past,
Finding only empty victories
    and a peace that cannot last.
But we've grown so rich and mighty
    and so arrogantly strong,
We no longer ask in humbleness—
    "God, show us where we're wrong."
We have come to trust completely
    in the power of man-made things,
Unmindful of God's mighty power
    and that He is King of kings.
We have turned our eyes away from Him
    to go our selfish way,

And money, power, and pleasure
    are the gods we serve today.
And the good green earth God gave us
    to peacefully enjoy,
Through greed and fear and hatred
    we are seeking to destroy.
O Father, up in heaven,
    stir and wake our sleeping souls,
Renew our faith and lift us up
    and give us higher goals,
And grant us heavenly guidance
    as Christmas comes again—
For more than guided missiles,
    all the world needs guided men.

Helen Steiner Rice
Christmas, 1961

*T*his is more than a card at the end of the year
Coming to wish you the season's good cheer,
It's a message of thanks I find hard to convey
For there's so little space and so much to say,
For so many people in so many ways
Have put new encouragement into my days
I just can't help thinking, and frequently too,
How grateful I am to know people like you.
And this truly has been a most wonderful year
With wonderful tributes from folks far and near,
Letters of praise, so kindly expressed,
I just can't help feeling both humble and blest,
For only God, working through people like you,
Could answer my prayers and make all this true,
For the people I meet and work with and see
Inspire the things which are written by me,
And the beauty folks find in a word, phrase, or line
Is their soul's reflection just mirrored in mine.
There's no time like Christmas with its meaningfulness
To recall and remember and attempt to express
How much it has meant through the year "sixty-two"
To have known and been helped by people like you,
And I hope God will bless you as we start "sixty-three"
And return all the kindness you've shown people like me.

Helen Steiner Rice
Christmas, 1962

$\mathcal{N}$othing would make me happier
    or please me any better
Than to write you my thanks
    in a long, friendly letter—
For being remembered
    at the holiday season
By someone like you
    gave my heart ample reason
To count all my blessings,
    and your friendship is one,
For without fans and friends
    the writing I've done
Would lose all its meaning,
    its warmth, and sincereness,
For how could I write
    without feeling a nearness
To all the dear people
    who interpret each line
With their own love and kindness
    that becomes part of mine.
So more than you know
    I thank God up above
For fans, friends, and family
    and their gifts of love.

Helen Steiner Rice
January, 1967

*M*y Christmas gift
    is a gift of love,
Made of words that I borrow
    from our Father above.
He gives them to me
    and I give them to you
And through Him we meet
    and communicate too.
And as Christmas comes
    and another year ends
I thank God once more
    for my fans and my friends.
And may my future writings
    be most worthy of
Your fanship and friendship
    as we share in His love.

Helen Steiner Rice
Christmas, 1968

I am planning to walk
   on a path yet untrod,
Content that my future
   will be determined by God—
But it doesn't take Christmas
   to make me remember,
Nor are my good wishes
   confined to December—
But as day follows day
   and thought follows thought,
I'll think of the joy
   that your friendship has brought,
And may the books I have written
   and the words I have spoken
Be a spiritual bond . . .
   unchanged and unbroken.

                    Helen Steiner Rice
                    Christmas, 1970

The Glow
of Giving

Christmas is the glow of giving—
shoppers shopping, children gift making,
mothers cooking, grandmothers baking,
fathers tree trimming, families caring,
homeless remembered, heartfelt sharing.

VJR

*A*nd in that region there were shepherds out in the field, keeping watch over their flock by night. And an angel of the Lord appeared to them, and the glory of the Lord shone around them, and they were filled with fear.

And the angel said to them, "Be not afraid; for behold, I bring you good news of a great joy which will come to all the people; for to you is born this day in the city of David a Savior, who is Christ the Lord. And this will be a sign for you: you will find a babe wrapped in swaddling cloths and lying in a manger." And suddenly there was with the angel a multitude of the heavenly host praising God and saying,

"Glory to God in the highest,
and on earth peace among men with whom he is pleased!"

Luke 2:8–14

Giving

Christmas is a season of giving,
And giving is the key to living.
So let us give ourselves away,
Not just at Christmas but every day
And remember a kind and thoughtful deed
Or a hand outstretched in time of need
Is the rarest of gifts for it is a part
Not of the purse but a loving heart,
And he who gives of himself will find
True joy of heart and peace of mind.

May the Gifts of Christmas Be Yours

The richest gifts
    are God's to give,
May you possess them
    as long as you live,
May you walk with Him
    and dwell in His love
As He sends you good gifts
    from heaven above.

Give Lavishly! Live Abundantly!

The more you give, the more you get,
The more you laugh, the less you fret,
The more you do unselfishly,
The more you live abundantly.

The more of everything you share,
The more you'll always have to spare,
The more you love, the more you'll find
That life is good and friends are kind.

For only what we give away,
Enriches us from day to day.
So let's live Christmas through the year
And fill the world with love and cheer.

The Christmas Tree

Listen . . . Be quiet . . . Perhaps you can hear the Christmas tree speaking . . . soft and clear:

I am God's messenger of love
   and in my Christmas dress,
I come to light your heart and home
   with joy and happiness.
I bring you pretty packages
   and longed-for gifts of love,
But most of all I bring you
   a message from above—
The message Christmas angels sang
   on that first Christmas night
When Jesus Christ, the Father's Son,
   became this dark world's light.
For though I'm tinsel laden
   and beautiful to see,

Remember, I am much, much more
   than just a glittering tree,
More than a decoration
   to enhance the Christmas scene,
I am a living symbol
   that God's love is ever green,
And when Christmas Day is over
   and the holidays are through,
May the joyous spirit of Christmas
   abide all year with you.
So have a Merry Christmas
   in the blessed Savior's name
And thank Him for the priceless gifts
   that are ours because He came.

A Christmas Prayer

Our Father who art in heaven,
  hear this Christmas prayer,
And if it be Thy gracious will
  may joy be everywhere—
The joy that comes from knowing
  that the holy Christ child came
To bless the earth at Christmas
  for Thy sake and in Thy name.
And with this prayer there comes a wish
  that these holy, happy days
Will bless you and your loved ones
  in many joyous ways.

Christmas Is a Season for Giving

Christmas is a season
    for gifts of every kind,
All the glittering, pretty things
    that Christmas shoppers find—
Baubles, beads, and bangles
    of silver and of gold—
Anything and everything
    that can be bought or sold
Is given at this season
    to place beneath the tree
For Christmas is a special time
    for giving lavishly,
But there's one rare and priceless gift
    that can't be sold or bought,
It's something poor or rich can give
    for it's a loving thought—
And loving thoughts are something
    for which no one can pay
And only loving hearts can give
    this priceless gift away.

Christmas Glitter

With our eyes
we see the glitter
of Christmas,
with our ears
we hear the merriment,
with our hands
we touch the
tinsel-tied trinkets,
but only
with our hearts
can we feel
the miracle of it.

The Gift of God's Love

All over the world at this season,
    expectant hands reach to receive
Gifts that are lavishly fashioned,
    the finest that man can conceive.
For purchased and given at Christmas
    are luxuries we long to possess,
Given as favors and tokens
    to try in some way to express
That strange, indefinable feeling
    that is part of this glad time of year
When streets are crowded with shoppers
    and the air resounds with good cheer.
But back of each tinsel-tied package
    exchanged at this gift-giving season,
Unrecognized often by many,
    lies a deeper, more meaningful reason,
For born in a manger at Christmas
    as a gift from the Father above,
An infant whose name was called Jesus
    brought mankind the gift of God's love.
And the gifts that we give have no purpose
    unless God is a part of the giving,
And unless we make Christmas a pattern
    to be followed in everyday living.

The Joy of Remembering

Christmas is the joy of remembering—
children sledding, groups ice-skating,
eyes twinkling, smiles radiating,
hot chocolate simmering, spirits glowing,
popcorn popping, snowflakes snowing,
fires in the hearth, burning and embering,
nostalgic memories, fond remembering.

VJR

*N*ow when Jesus was born in Bethlehem of Judea in the days of Herod the king, behold, wise men from the East came to Jerusalem, saying, "Where is he who has been born king of the Jews? For we have seen his star in the East, and have come to worship him." When Herod the king heard this, he was troubled, and all Jerusalem with him; and assembling all the chief priests and scribes of the people, he inquired of them where the Christ was to be born. They told him, "In Bethlehem of Judea; for so it is written by the prophet . . ."

When they had heard the king they went their way; and lo, the star which they had seen in the East went before them, till it came to rest over the place where the child was. When they saw the star, they rejoiced exceedingly with great joy; and going into the house they saw the child with Mary his mother, and they fell down and worshiped him. Then, opening their treasures, they offered him gifts, gold and frankincense and myrrh.

Matthew 2:1–5, 9–11

Rejoice! It's Christmas!

May the holy remembrance
    of the first Christmas Day
Be our reassurance
    Christ is not far away.
For on Christmas He came
    to walk here on earth,
So let us find joy
    in the news of His birth.
And let us find comfort
    and strength for each day
In knowing that Christ
    walked this same earthly way.
So He knows all our needs
    and He hears every prayer

And He keeps all His children
    always safe in His care.
And whenever we're troubled
    and lost in despair
We have but to seek Him
    and ask Him in prayer
To guide and direct us
    and help us to bear
Our sickness and sorrow,
    our worry and care.
So once more at Christmas
    let the whole world rejoice
In the knowledge He answers
    every prayer that we voice.

Christmas Is a Season of Kindness

May the kindly spirit of Christmas
    spread its radiance far and wide
So all the world may feel the glow
    of this holy Christmastide,
And then may every heart and home
    continue through the year
To feel the warmth and wonder
    of this season of good cheer,
And may it bring us closer
    to God and to each other
'Til every stranger is a friend,
    and every man a brother.

Christmas and the Christ Child

In our Christmas celebrations
  of merriment and mirth,
Let's not forget the miracle
  of the holy Christ child's birth,
For in our festivities
  it is easy to lose sight
Of the baby in the manger
  and that holy silent night.
And we miss the mighty meaning
  and we lose the greater glory
Of the holy little Christ child
  and the blessed Christmas story
If we don't keep Christ in Christmas
  and make His love a part
Of all the joy and happiness
  that fill our home and heart.

The Presence of Jesus

Jesus came into this world
   one glorious Christmas Eve.
He came to live right here on earth
   to help us to believe.
For God up in His heaven
   knew His children all would feel
That if Jesus lived among them
   they would know that He was real
And not a far-off stranger
   who dwelt up in the sky
And knew neither joys nor sorrows
   that make us laugh and cry.
And so He walked among us
   and taught us how to love
And promised us that someday we
   would dwell with Him above.
And while we cannot see Him
   as they did, face to face,
We know that He is everywhere,
   not in some far-off place.

Keep Christ in Christmas

If we keep Christ in Christmas
  He will keep us every day,
And when we are in His keeping
  and we follow in His way,
All our little earthly sorrows,
  all our worry and our care
Seem lifted from our shoulders
  when we go to God in prayer.

This Is the Savior of the World

Some regard the Christmas story
    as something beautiful to hear,
A lovely Christmas custom
    that we celebrate each year.
But it's more than just a story
    told to make our hearts rejoice,
It's our Father up in heaven
    speaking through the Christ child's voice
Telling us of heavenly kingdoms
    that He has prepared above
For those who put their trust
    in His mercy and His love.
And only through the Christ child
    can man be born again,
For God sent the baby Jesus
    as the Savior of all men.

Let Us Pray
on This Holy Christmas Day

What better time
  and what better season,
What greater occasion
  or more wonderful reason
To kneel down in prayer
  and lift our hands high
To the God of creation,
  who made land and sky.
And, oh, what a privilege
  as the new year begins
To ask God to wipe out
  our errors and sins
And to know when we ask,
  if we are sincere,
He will wipe our slate clean
  as we start a new year.
So at this glad season
  when joy's everywhere,
Let us meet our Redeemer
  at the altar of prayer.

My Wish

Show me the way,
   not to fortune and fame,
Not how to win laurels
   or praise for my name—
But show me the way
   to spread the great story,
That Thine is the kingdom
   and power and glory.

HSR

My Hope

Christmas encompasses all you've just read—
   but the very special part
      is glorifying God
   by the service of your life
      and the thanks within your heart.

VJR